Eat smart, Live Lean: The Roadmap to Eating Right, Staying Fit, and Feeling Great

Table of Contents

Introduction 1

Chapter 1: Why Health Starts With Diet 4

Chapter 2: Understanding Processed vs Unprocessed Foods ... 8

Chapter 3: The Problems of Sugar and Addictive Ingredients 16

Chapter 4: Breaking Bad Habits and Building New Ones 25

Chapter 5: Step by Step Guide to Dietary Transition 31

Chapter 6: Exercise and Its Role in Health 38

Chapter 7: Setting Goals and Tracking Progress 47

Chapter 8: The Power of Sleep and Its Impact on Health 51

Chapter 9: The Benefits of Healthy Fasting Habits 58

Chapter 10: Managing Stress for Better Health 65

Chapter 11: Supplements and Nutrient Essentials 73

Chapter 12: Staying Consistent 80

Chapter 13: Having a Balanced Lifestyle Without Feeling Deprived... 85

Chapter 14: Self-reflection and Setting Goals 90

Chapter 15: Creating a Roadmap... 94

Introduction

Welcome to your easy guide for unlocking a healthier, happier you! This book is your inviting companion on a transformative journey, designed to reshape your relationship with food, fitness, and overall wellness in a way that feels simple, practical, and downright enjoyable. Think of it as your friendly roadmap, guiding you through the why and how of making nourishing choices that not only benefit your body but also become comforting habits you can carry with you for life.

We'll start by diving into the essentials: understanding food. You'll discover the magic of real, unprocessed foods, unravel why they are essential for your well-being and learn to distinguish between options that fuel your vitality and those that leave you feeling sluggish. But we won't stop there. We'll explore the world of habits. Unpacking why those tempting sugary snacks seem so irresistible and how you can artfully shift those cravings towards healthier delights without feeling deprived.

And that's just the tip of the iceberg! The book will walk you through personalised exercise routines that resonate with you, help you set realistic goals, and cultivate a mindset that champions lasting transformation. We'll delve into crucial aspects like the significance of sleep, effective stress management techniques, and gently introduce you to the idea of fasting if it aligns with your health journey.

Each chapter is crafted to build on the previous one, ensuring that by the end of your reading, you're equipped with a comprehensive toolkit for sustainable health.

With straightforward advice, relatable anecdotes, and a sprinkle of humour, this book promises to make your journey to better health not just achievable but enjoyable too. Forget about drastic overhauls. Get ready to embrace tiny yet impactful changes that result in remarkable outcomes. Whether your goal is to shed some weight, boost your energy levels, or simply regain control of your wellness, this book will be your ally in crafting the vibrant, fulfilling life you truly deserve.

Chapter 1: Why Health Starts With Diet

Let's kick things off with a powerful truth: your body is complex, an engine of life that needs the right fuel to operate at its best. Think of it like this. When you eat high quality food, your body hums along beautifully. But fill it with junk, and it's like watching a car break down. Food is your fuel, and it's essential to remember that not all food is created equal.

At the heart of nutrition are three macronutrients. carbohydrates, proteins, and fats. Each playing a crucial role in keeping your body running smoothly. Carbohydrates are your body's go to source of energy. They break down into glucose, powering everything from your brain to your workouts. You can think of them as the sprinting champion of the nutrient world. Fast and efficient! But here's the catch, not all carbs are created equal. Try to eat whole grains, fruits, and vegetables to get the good stuff, while sugary snacks and processed carbs are just empty calories that won't do you any favours.

Let's talk about proteins. These are your body's repair crew, tirelessly rebuilding muscles, supporting tissues, and fortifying your immune system. Lean meats, beans, and nuts are excellent sources of protein that your body craves. Then come the fats often misunderstood but absolutely essential for hormone production and sustained energy. Embrace healthy fats found in avocados, olive oil, and fatty fish, while steering clear of processed options.

Micronutrients, vitamins and minerals are the unsung heroes in this equation. Vitamins like A, C, and D are vital for everything from boosting your immunity to supporting bone health. Minerals like calcium and iron are key for strong bones and oxygen rich blood. You can easily get these from supplements, but why not indulge in whole foods? fruits and vegetables are nature's multivitamins and provide the best sources of these nutrients.

Once food enters your system, it embarks on an amazing journey. Chewed and broken down in your stomach, it's absorbed in your small intestine and sent off to nourish your cells, providing energy, repair materials, or storage for later. Every bite has an impact, food fuels your energy, influences your mood, and even affects hormones like serotonin and cortisol. A balanced, nutrient rich meal can leave you energised and happy, while sugary or overly processed foods can reduce your energy and make you feel irritable.

Make sure to have a mix of carbs, proteins, and healthy fats, and never underestimate the power of variety. Stay hydrated, water is crucial for nearly every process in your body. Remember, food is about more than just fuel; it's an experience filled with joy and connection. Choose wisely, savour the journey, and enjoy the process. After all, your body is a miracle, and nourishing it is one of the best gifts you can give yourself!

Not all Foods are Created Equal

Picture this: two apples. One is plucked fresh from the tree, crisp and juicy, nearly bursting with nature's pure goodness. The other? Well, it's undergone quite a transformation: sweetened, heated, canned, and morphed into something that barely resembles an apple. It's more "product" than fruit. This, my friends, is where the great debate over processed versus unprocessed foods begins.

Processed foods have strayed far from their original forms. They're toys for food scientists, often packed with additives, preservatives, sugars, and artificial colours designed to enhance flavour, extend shelf life, or just make them look attractive on shop shelves. Think of crisps, instant noodles, sugary cereals, and fizzy drinks. Convenient, yes, but mostly in flashy packaging that distracts from what's inside. On the flip side, unprocessed foods are as close to nature as it gets. We're talking about fruits, crisp vegetables, hearty whole grains, nutritious nuts, and lean meats. Simple, honest, and absolutely no fuss. They don't need marketing hype or a laundry list of unrecognisable ingredients; they're just real food.

So why should we care? The way food is processed can dramatically affect its nutritional value and its impact on our bodies. A diet heavy in processed items is often linked to various health problems, from unwanted weight gain to energy crashes. In contrast, unprocessed foods deliver nutrients in their natural state. Exactly what our bodies are designed to utilise.

We're embarking on an eye-opening journey to explore the major differences between these two food realms. We'll uncover the hidden surprises lurking in processed options and reveal why embracing unprocessed foods is the key to unlocking better health. Let's dive into the captivating world of food in all its natural and, yes, not so natural forms.

Chapter 2: Understanding Processed vs Unprocessed Foods

Processed Foods

Welcome to the world of processed foods where convenience meets health risks, and the truth can be quite unsettling. So, what exactly are these processed foods? Picture anything that's strayed from its natural state, either to tantalise our taste buds, extend shelf life, or make meals quicker and easier. This spectrum ranges from the relatively innocent (think frozen vegetables) to the downright dubious like those bright, neon cheese puffs that bear little resemblance to real food. While food manufacturers aim to create products that are a breeze to produce and consume, the hidden cost might just be your wellbeing.

Let's delve into what really makes processed foods unhealthy. Sugar is a major culprit, lurking in everything from your morning cereal to sneaky salad dressings. But sugar isn't just a little extra sweetness; it's an addictive substance that lights up your brain like a Christmas tree. Each time you indulge, your brain releases dopamine, the "feel good" hormone, sending you down a slippery slope of craving more. This sweet rollercoaster can lead to weight gain, volatile blood sugar levels, and even unpredictable mood shifts. It's no surprise we keep reaching for those sugary snacks, they've been carefully crafted to keep us coming back for more!

Next up on the ingredients list is preservatives. These chemicals help keep our food from spoiling, but they come with a hidden price tag. Take BHA and BHT, for instance, common preservatives that may extend shelf life but could also put your health at risk. They can trigger inflammation, weight gain or even serious chronic diseases over time. And let's be honest, trying to avoid preservatives in processed foods is like trying to dodge raindrops in a storm.

Now, let's shine a light on artificial colours and flavours. They're the flashy sidekicks trying to make junk food more enticing, but they don't offer a single nutrient. In fact, some artificial colours are linked to hyperactivity in children, potential allergic reactions and other health issues. It's astonishing to think that many of these additives are banned in certain countries.

And we can't overlook the fats lurking in processed foods. Many are loaded with unhealthy trans fats and unhealthy oils, all for that irresistible texture and extended shelf life. But these trans fats do more harm than good, they raise bad cholesterol levels, clog arteries, and heighten your risk of heart disease. While they may enhance that crunch or creamy mouthfeel, your heart will certainly pay the price in the long run.

So, how do these foods affect our brains and bodies? Prepare for an energy rollercoaster! Ever noticed how you're on a high after a sugary treat only to come crashing down shortly afterwards? That's your body grappling with the rapid spikes and crashes in blood sugar caused by processed carbohydrates and sugars. Over time, these energetic spikes can leave you feeling fatigued and irritable, and perhaps even anxious. As your blood sugar fluctuates, your energy levels struggle to keep pace, resulting in that drained feeling we all dread.

Your brain, a delicate powerhouse, is particularly vulnerable to the effects of processed foods. Diets rich in sugar and unhealthy fats can contribute to cognitive decline and mental health challenges like depression and anxiety. Without the essential nutrients like omega-3s, antioxidants, and vitamins, your brain can't function at its best. Instead of feeling sharp and alert, you might find yourself in a foggy, sluggish state as if your brain is operating on low battery.

Finally, let's address the addictive nature of these foods. They're engineered to be hyper palatable, expertly combining sugar, salt, and fat to hit that sweet "bliss point" that makes it nearly impossible to resist. This trickery can lead to overindulgence, making it hard to maintain portion control and eventually resulting in weight gain and health repercussions.

In a nutshell, while processed foods might be quick and appetising, they come with a hefty list of potential health risks. They throw your body off balance and complicate your relationship with food. The next time you reach for that bright bag of snacks, take a moment to consider what you're really putting into your body. Your health will thank you!

Unprocessed Foods

Imagine this: your body is like a vibrant garden, full of potential. To truly thrive, it needs the right elements, rich soil, bright sunlight, and refreshing water. Neglect it or sprinkle in some junk, and you'll be left with drooping plants and bare patches. Just as a garden flourishes when nurtured with pure, natural ingredients, your body blooms with the goodness of unprocessed foods. These gems often referred to as "whole foods" are untouched by the manufacturing process, existing in their natural, wholesome state. Think of fresh fruits and vegetables, whole grains, lean meats, fish, eggs, and nuts. They're nature's bounty, offering a treasure trove of benefits for both mind and body.

Let's delve into why unprocessed foods are so exceptional. These powerhouses are filled with vitamins, minerals, fibre, and antioxidants. Consider the vibrancy of fresh produce: imagine leafy greens, succulent berries, crunchy carrots, and colourful bell peppers. They're not just visually appealing; they pack a serious nutritional punch. Loaded with vitamins such as A, C, and E, and essential minerals like potassium and magnesium, these foods don't just fill you up, they fuel your cells, supercharge your organs, and improve your immune system. In contrast, processed foods often lose these vital nutrients, leaving you feeling deprived.

Now, let's explore the magic unprocessed foods can work for your brain. Despite making up just a small percentage of your body weight, your brain consumes a staggering 20% of your energy! To stay sharp, it requires continuous access to nutrients that enhance clarity, focus, and memory. Enter unprocessed foods, the ultimate fuel for your mental engine. Leafy greens are rich in folate and omega-3 fatty acids from foods like salmon and walnuts support your brain cell structure. Conversely, processed snacks loaded with sugar and unhealthy fats can lead to mental fog and even mood swings. Feeding your brain unprocessed foods is like giving it a refreshing tune up, keeping it sharp and eager to tackle the day.

Unprocessed foods also power your physical health in remarkable ways. Lean meats, fish, eggs, and legumes are fantastic sources of high-quality protein. This is what your body needs to build muscle, repair tissues, and create vital enzymes and hormones. Choosing these unprocessed proteins means equipping your muscles with the tools they need for recovery and growth, whether you're lifting weights or simply going through your daily routine. Plus, natural protein sources are more filling, helping you feel satisfied longer, which is a major plus if you're looking to maintain a healthy weight.

Don't overlook the incredible benefits of dietary fibre as well. Found in whole grains, fruits, and vegetables, fibre acts like a broom for your digestive system, sweeping away waste and keeping everything running smoothly. It regulates blood sugar levels, keeps you feeling full, and helps lower cholesterol. Unfortunately, in the quest for tastier processed foods, fibre is often stripped away, leading to sluggish digestion and increased risk of heart disease. By prioritising unprocessed, fibre rich choices, you're investing in not just gut health, but your overall well-being.

Let's shine a light on antioxidants, abundant allies in unprocessed foods, particularly in fruits and vegetables. Think of antioxidants as the bodyguards of your cells, shielding them from harmful free radicals, unstable molecules that can accelerate ageing and disease. Berries, for instance, are packed with powerful antioxidants like anthocyanins that reduce inflammation and enhance brain function. A diet rich in these natural defenders can help lower your risk of chronic diseases and strengthen your body's immune system, keeping you vibrant and healthy.

And perhaps the best part? The impact unprocessed foods can have on your mood and energy levels. You know that feeling when you finish a fresh, balanced meal, energised and content? Now compare that to the sluggishness that follows a heavy, processed meal. Unprocessed foods provide a steady release of energy, keeping your blood sugar balanced and your spirits elevated throughout the day. Complex carbohydrates in whole grains digest slowly, ensuring lasting energy instead of the peaks and troughs from sugary snacks. Stable energy levels benefit not just your body, but also your mind, helping you avoid irritability and fatigue.

In a nutshell, unprocessed foods are a powerhouse for brain and body vitality. They offer essential nutrients, support your energy levels, assist muscle growth and recovery, promote gut health, protect your cells, and nurture your overall well-being. Choose wisely, and let your body thrive like the flourishing garden it was meant to be.

Unprocessed Foods and Weight Control

One of the standout benefits of unprocessed foods is their impressive fibre content. Fibre is like your digestive system's best friend; it slows down digestion, helping you feel satisfied for longer and keeping those pesky cravings at bay. Foods like whole grains, leafy greens, and beans are fibre powerhouses that help stabilise your blood sugar levels, so you won't experience those dreaded energy crashes that usually lead to mindless snacking. On the flip side, processed snacks can spike your blood sugar like a rollercoaster, leaving you feeling hungry again in no time.

But there's even more! Unprocessed foods also require more energy for your body to break them down, a phenomenon known as the "thermic effect" of food. Simply put, your body burns more calories digesting wholesome foods than it does tackling processed ones. Imagine your body working overtime to digest a succulent piece of lean chicken or a nourishing bowl of quinoa, consider it a little workout that supports your weight management journey over time.

Unprocessed foods can help keep your metabolism balanced and cravings in check. When you fill your plate with nutrient dense meals, your body gets all the vitamins, minerals, and macronutrients it craves. In contrast, processed foods are often loaded with sugars and unhealthy fats that can leave your brain wanting more, even when you've had enough. By embracing unprocessed foods, you equip your body with everything it needs to thrive, making it easier to control portion sizes, avoid overeating, and maintain a healthy weight that feels sustainable and enjoyable.

Chapter 3: The Problems of Sugar and Addictive Ingredients

Sugar is the Enemy

Sugar is everywhere, sneaking into not just sweets but also everyday foods like sauces, bread, and even those so called "healthy" snacks. While it might make things taste delightful, sugar is a significant culprit behind weight gain and a host of health issues that can impact both your body and mind. So, what's really happening when you indulge in sugary treats?

Imagine taking a sip of a fizzy drink or biting into a chocolate bar. In no time, your blood sugar levels spike, sending your body into action. It releases insulin, a crucial hormone that helps regulate blood sugar by ushering glucose from your bloodstream into your cells. While insulin plays a vital role, consuming too much sugar forces your body to churn out more insulin to keep everything in check, leading to a rollercoaster of highs and lows in your blood sugar levels.

As this cycle continues, your body starts storing more fat, particularly around your midsection. Why? Insulin acts like a "storage hormone," making it simpler for your body to stash away energy as fat instead of burning it off. This winding path can lead to weight gain and, eventually, insulin resistance, where your cells become less responsive to insulin. This resistance is a stepping stone to type 2 diabetes, a chronic condition closely linked to obesity and excessive sugar intake.

One of the sneakiest things about sugar is that it provides so called "empty calories." Foods packed with added sugars usually have little to offer beyond their calorie count. A sugary snack might give you a quick energy spike, but it won't keep you satisfied or provide the protein, fibre, or healthy fats your body craves. That's why you often find yourself hungry again shortly after indulging in sweet treats, leading to more cravings and potentially overeating. On top of that, sugar triggers a rush of dopamine, the "feel good" hormone in the brain. This sugar fuelled high is fleeting, leaving you wanting more, much like an addiction. This beautiful yet treacherous cycle of craving and consumption can derail your efforts to maintain a healthy weight.

Sugar also plays tricks on your metabolism in more subtle ways. Take fructose, a common type of sugar found in many processed foods; it doesn't metabolise the same way as glucose, the sugar your body efficiently uses for energy. While nearly every cell can utilise glucose, fructose is mainly processed by the liver. Consuming an abundance of fructose can overwhelm your liver, which then turns the excess into fat. Over time, this can lead to non-alcoholic fatty liver disease (NAFLD), a troubling condition where fat accumulates in the liver, compromising its functionality. The fat doesn't just sit there; it enters your bloodstream, making it even more difficult to shed those unwanted pounds.

Regular consumption is associated with mood swings, irritability, and even anxiety and depression. Why? Sugar alters brain chemistry. As we discussed, it prompts dopamine release, giving you a fleeting sense of pleasure. But when that sugar high fades away, you may find yourself crashing and feeling tired, cranky, or down. This emotional rollercoaster is compounded by sugar's effect on blood sugar levels. When those levels drop after a high-sugar dose, you're likely to experience a "sugar crash," leaving you fighting fatigue and mood dips. Over time, this cycle breeds chronic fatigue and emotional turbulence.

The long-term repercussions of high sugar intake stretch far beyond just weight gain and energy dips. Chronic sugar consumption is linked to an increased risk of severe health conditions like heart disease, diabetes, and even some cancers.

Consistently high blood sugar levels can damage blood vessels, heightening the risk of cardiovascular problems, while obesity and insulin resistance pose major threats for type 2 diabetes. On top of that, indulging in sugary treats can weaken your immune system. Yes, studies have shown that stuffing down excessive sugar can temporarily impair your immune function, making it harder for your body to fend off illnesses. Over time, this weakened immunity means a high sugar diet can leave you more vulnerable to becoming unwell.

So, cutting back on sugar isn't merely about trimming calories; it's about breaking a cycle that affects your entire body, from metabolism to weight management and mental well-being. Reducing your sugar intake can help stabilise blood sugar levels, ease cravings, and support a healthier weight overall. As you gradually scale back, you may find yourself bursting with more energy, feeling in a better mood, and experiencing fewer health issues. Plus, cutting sugar opens the door to a world of nutrient rich foods that genuinely nourish your body and promote overall wellness.

Sugar is far more than just an innocent indulgence, it's a major player in weight gain and a disruptor of metabolic health. By becoming aware and making conscious choices, you can pave the way for a healthier, happier you.

The Other Addictive Ingredients

Behind the scenes, a roster of addictive ingredients works together like a well-rehearsed symphony to create irresistible snacks and meals. The food industry has become a master at combining salt, unhealthy fats, artificial flavourings, and preservatives, making it all too easy to get hooked. Each of these components plays a pivotal role in igniting cravings, promoting overeating, and trapping us in a cycle that can sap our energy and jeopardise our health. Let's take a closer look at these enticing ingredients, their effects on our bodies, and why they make processed foods so tantalisingly hard to resist.

First up is salt. While our bodies do need some sodium, processed foods are often overloaded with it. Salt isn't just a seasoning; it's a flavour enhancer that makes food taste rich and satisfying. Over time, a diet high in salt can alter your taste buds, conditioning you to crave ever-saltier snacks. After feasting on salty treats, fresh fruits and vegetables can taste downright bland. Your brain begins to prefer that intense saltiness, leading you right back to crisps, crackers, and other processed goodies. But beware: this craving for salt isn't just about taste. Excessive sodium can raise your blood pressure and increase your risk of heart disease. Plus, those salty meals can leave you feeling bloated and sluggish, draining your energy and motivation.

Next, let's explore unhealthy fats, particularly trans fats and refined vegetable oils. Trans fats, often lurking in fried foods and baked goods are artificially created to enhance texture and extend shelf life. They might stabilise food products, but they come with a hefty price tag on your health, spiking your bad cholesterol and lowering good cholesterol. As if that weren't enough, trans fats can be downright addictive, triggering dopamine release in your brain similar to sugar. This creates a vicious cycle where you find yourself endlessly reaching for those satisfying, high fat snacks.

Then we have refined vegetable oils, think soybean, corn, and canola oil. These inexpensive oils dominate processed foods but harbour a hidden danger: they contain high levels of omega-6 fatty acids. While we do need some omega-6 in our diets, too much can lead to inflammation and a host of health problems, from joint pain to heart disease. What's more, unhealthy fats are packed with calories but don't fill you up effectively, leaving you hungrier for more and more.

Artificial flavourings are another secret weapon in the allure of processed foods. When snacks are artificially flavoured, they're crafted to provide an incredibly intense and appealing taste experience. Have you ever noticed how "cheese" flavour in crisps can taste nothing like real cheese? That's because these flavours are engineered in labs to entice our taste buds like no natural food can. This exaggerated flavour can dull the appeal of whole, unprocessed foods, making them feel bland in comparison. Plus, artificial flavours can disrupt your body's hunger signals, leading to overeating without you even realising it.

And let's not forget about preservatives, like monosodium glutamate (MSG), which are often added to boost flavour even further. MSG stimulates the taste buds, creating a flavour explosion that's nearly impossible to resist. This intense satisfaction encourages you to eat more than you actually need. To top it off, MSG has been known to trigger insulin release, which can lead to blood sugar crashes and a renewed sense of hunger shortly after eating.

In a nutshell, these addictive ingredients work in tandem to create a whirlwind of flavours and sensations that keep us reaching for processed foods, often to the detriment of our health. Recognising their impact is the first step toward making more mindful, health-conscious choices.

Practical Ways to Reduce Your Sugar Intake

Cutting back on sugar doesn't have to feel like a punishment! In fact, it can be an empowering journey towards healthier living. One of the most effective ways to start is by uncovering the sneaky places sugar hides in our food. You'd be surprised to find sugar lurking in items that don't even taste sweet. The next time you're at the supermarket, grab that product label and scrutinise it for added sugars listed under names like "sucrose," "glucose," "high-fructose corn syrup," or even "cane juice." By becoming more aware of these ingredients, you can make savvy choices, swapping out those high-sugar culprits for delicious lower sugar or unsweetened alternatives. These small tweaks can be your golden ticket to a healthier lifestyle.

Let's not forget about drinks! Sugary beverages like energy drinks, and sweetened coffees can pack as much sugar as a handful of biscuits in just one serving. To tackle this, try reducing your intake slowly. Ditch the cola for refreshing sparkling water with a splash of lemon, lime or mix fruit juice with water for a lighter option. Explore the world of unsweetened teas, herbal infusions, or water infused with fresh fruit. You might be surprised at how satisfying these choices can be and how your taste buds start to adapt to less sweetness over time.

If you're in the habit of sweetening your coffee, yoghurt, or porridge, why not experiment with natural flavourings? A sprinkle of cinnamon or a dash of vanilla can elevate your dish without the sugar overload. Mashed bananas or berries can sweeten up your meals naturally, steering clear of those dreaded blood sugar spikes. And while dates can add a delightful sweetness, remember that moderation is key, even with natural sweeteners!

Now, let's talk about enjoying desserts. Instead of bidding farewell to your favourite sweet treats, try savouring smaller portions. If you usually devour an entire chocolate bar, why not start with half? Or swap a hefty slice of cake for a tiny piece of dark chocolate after dinner. You might just find that smaller portions are surprisingly satisfying, letting you indulge your sweet tooth without overdoing it on sugar.

One big reason we crave sugar is due to fluctuating blood sugar levels, often caused by skipping meals or eating imbalanced ones. By focusing on regular, balanced meals complete with a mix of protein, healthy fats, and fibre you can keep those cravings at bay. Think of a hearty breakfast with eggs, avocado, and wholegrain toast. By nurturing your body with nutrient-rich meals, you'll find it easier to resist those sugary snacks.

When you feel that sweet craving coming on, reach for a piece of fresh fruit instead of a processed treat. Fruits are packed with natural sugars, vitamins, and fibre making them a far healthier choice. The fibre in fruit helps slow sugar absorption, offering your body a steady release of energy. Try different fruits like juicy apples, vibrant berries, or refreshing melons and you might discover that fresh fruit can satisfy your cravings just as well as those sugary snacks without the empty calories.

Cooking at home is another powerful way to take control of your sugar intake. Cooking allows you to dictate what goes into your meals, ensuring you know exactly how much sugar you're consuming. Restaurant dishes and pre-packaged foods are often loaded with hidden sugars, but at home, you can experiment by cutting sugar in your favourite recipes or substituting it with natural options like mashed bananas. Savvy modifications like these can lead to mouthwatering meals that are low in added sugars.

Sometimes, we reach for sugar out of habit or as a coping mechanism rather than actual hunger. This is where mindful eating comes into play. Before you grab that sugary snack, take a moment to pause and assess whether you're truly hungry or if you're responding to boredom, stress, or a low mood. By tuning into your body's signals, you can recognise when those sugar habits kick in and find healthier ways to cope, whether that's going for a walk, diving into a good book, or catching up with a friend.

Remember, reducing sugar doesn't have to be an all or nothing mission. Start small with achievable goals. Perhaps you could cut the sugar in your coffee by half, or limit dessert to just a few nights a week. As you gain confidence with each little victory, you can tackle bigger goals. These incremental steps make managing your sugar intake easier and more enjoyable, plus, it's essential to celebrate every bit of progress! Embrace the change and live a better life.

Chapter 4: Breaking Bad Habits and Building New Ones

Have you ever thought about how habits shape your everyday life? They're like mental shortcuts that help your brain save energy by automating repetitive actions. Remember how you don't have to give a second thought to brushing your teeth or tying your shoelaces? Once a behaviour turns into a habit, it becomes hardwired in your brain, making it effortless to repeat. While this can work wonders for positive habits, it can also spell trouble for less healthy choices, like reaching for junk food during stressful times or getting lost in your phone instead of heading to bed. The great news? By understanding how habits function in our brains, you can reshape them and make healthier choices.

At the heart of every habit is something called the "habit loop," which consists of three crucial parts: the cue, the routine, and the reward. The cue acts as a trigger for your brain, signalling that it's time to dive into the habit. This trigger can be anything from seeing a tempting treat to feeling stressed or bored. Then comes the routine, the actual behaviour itself, like munching on that treat. Finally, there's the reward: the satisfying benefit you gain from the action, whether it's the immediate pleasure from a snack or a break from stress. This reward reinforces the habit loop, making it more likely that you'll go through the same motions when the cue pops up again.

But what if you want to change that habit? The secret lies in understanding and modifying this loop. Rather than trying to eliminate a habit completely, something that can be quite challenging, focus on altering the routine while keeping the same cue and reward. For example, if your habit is to snack when stress hits then consider taking a quick walk instead or drink a glass of water to supress the hunger. You're still addressing the stress cue and enjoying a reward, but in a way that's healthier for you.

A fantastic technique to help rewire your habits is called "implementation intention." It's all about crafting a specific plan for when and where you will engage in your new habit. Rather than a vague ambition like "I want to eat better," try something concrete: "When I want to snack, I will choose a piece of fruit instead." By setting up this detailed plan, you're programming your brain to respond to the cue with a clear action, leading to greater success in establishing those healthier habits.

Another exciting aspect of rewiring your brain is the concept of "neuroplasticity." This is your brain's incredible ability to reorganise itself by forming new neural connections throughout your life. Each time you repeat a positive behaviour, you strengthen the neural pathways linked to that action, making it easier and more automatic over time. Imagine walking on a grassy path, each time you take that same route, the path becomes clearer and easier to follow. The more you practise a healthy habit, the stronger that neural pathway grows, while the weaker, old pathways associated with unhealthy choices fade.

However, remember that rewiring habits isn't an overnight miracle; it requires patience and consistency. Research indicates that adopting a new habit can take several weeks to months, depending on how complicated the change is. During this journey, it's completely normal to face setbacks, especially when the old habit feels more familiar. The key is to keep going, even if you stumble occasionally. Each time you embrace that new behaviour, you're reinforcing the pathway, making it easier for your brain to choose the healthier option down the line.

Additionally, consider focusing on "identity-based habits." Rather than fixating on the outcome you want, think about the person you aspire to become. Instead of merely aiming to "exercise more," start seeing yourself as someone who values fitness and health. When you identify with that mindset, the habit becomes part of who you are, making it easier to stay committed. When faced with a choice, ask yourself questions like, "What would a healthy person do?" or "Is this decision aligned with my goal of becoming healthier?" This alignment deepens the reinforcement of your new habits.

To make things even easier, start with small, manageable changes that won't feel overwhelming. This approach, often called "habit stacking," involves adding a new, tiny habit onto an existing one, making it easier to remember and achieve. For instance, if you want to increase your water intake, link it to an established routine, like drinking a glass of water every time you brush your teeth.

By embracing these strategies, you can take control of your habits and guide your brain towards healthier choices.

Breaking the Habit Cycle

Start by tuning into your own behaviours. Spend a few days observing your routines without any judgement. If you're trying to cut back on unhealthy snacking, write down when and why you snack. Are you reaching for that sugary treat because you're bored or just plain hungry? Understanding your triggers is the first crucial step to making meaningful changes. Once you know what drives you, set clear and specific goals. Instead of the vague statement, "I want to eat healthier," opt for something concrete like, "I'll swap my afternoon snack for a piece of fruit three times a week." This way, you have a clear map guiding you towards success!

Remember, attempting to tackle too many changes at once can lead to burnout and frustration. Focus on one habit at a time and give yourself a few weeks to really embrace it. Let's say your first focus is drinking more water. Make that your sole priority until it feels second nature. Once that habit is firmly established, you can build on it by integrating more vegetables into your diet. Taking this gradual approach not only makes each change more manageable but also lays a strong foundation for lasting transformation.

Instead of fixating on cutting out unhealthy habits entirely, try replacing them with healthier options. This doesn't just prevent feelings of deprivation; it also helps you stay committed to your goals. For example, when you're stressed or tired and used to grabbing sugary snacks, opt for a handful of nuts, a piece of fruit, or some yoghurt instead. If you're aiming to reduce screen time before bed, swap it out for a soothing activity like reading or practising mindfulness. By discovering satisfying alternatives, you create a positive experience that makes the new habit far easier to maintain.

Preparation is key for those moments that challenge your resolve. Using "if-then" planning can be incredibly beneficial. For instance, if you're trying to avoid sugary drinks, you might decide, "If I feel like buying a soda, then I'll have sparkling water with lemon instead." This proactive planning helps you to mentally prepare for potential triggers and reinforces healthier choices, making it simpler to stick with your new habits. Over time, these responses become automatic, effectively strengthening your new routine.

Starting with smaller goals can be a game-changer! If you're looking to establish a regular exercise routine, begin with just five or ten minutes each day instead of a daunting hour. As you adjust, you can gradually increase the time or intensity of your workouts. The same applies to dietary changes; instead of overhauling your entire meals, add an extra serving of vegetables to just one meal each day. These small wins boost your confidence and prevent feelings of overwhelm, integrating new habits into your daily life effortlessly.

Tracking your progress is vital as it reinforces your commitment and adds a layer of motivation. Consider keeping a journal, using a diet tracking app, or simply checking off each day you stick to your new habit. Not only does tracking help you identify patterns, but it also allows you to celebrate small wins along the way. Reward yourself for achieving these milestones, perhaps treat yourself to a movie night or an hour of relaxation instead of a sugary dessert. Just ensure that your reward aligns with your overall goals!

Lastly, surround yourself with a supportive environment. If your aim is healthier eating, stock up on nutritious snacks and minimise junk food at home. Looking to be more active? Find a friend to join you for walks or workouts. Surrounding yourself with positive influences, whether through social media or communities dedicated to healthy lifestyles can provide the motivation and accountability you need to stay on track. A little encouragement goes a long way in keeping you focused on your goals.

Chapter 5: Step by Step Guide to Dietary Transition

Transitioning to a healthier diet doesn't have to be a chore! With a gradual approach, you can make lasting changes that feel effortless and enjoyable. This week-by-week guide is packed with simple steps to help you swap out unhealthy foods for nourishing options.

Week 1: Refresh Your Beverages

Let's kick things off by tackling what you drink! Sugary beverages like fizzy drinks and energy drinks are sneaky culprits of empty calories. This week, start replacing those sugary sips with refreshing alternatives. If you love sweetening your coffee or tea, why not try cutting back the sugar to half? By the end of the week, aim for at least 50% of your beverages to be wholesome water or other unsweetened delights. This step will leave you feeling hydrated and energised.

Week 2: Revamp Your Breakfast

Time to transform your mornings! If your breakfast usually involves sugary cereals or pastries, swap them out for hearty, nutritious options. How about creamy porridge topped with fresh fruit and nuts or avocado toast with a perfectly boiled egg? Whip up smoothies with vibrant fruits and greens for a delicious morning boost! By fuelling up with protein, fibre, and healthy fats, you'll stay full and focused until lunch.

Week 3: Give Snacks a Makeover

It's snack time, but let's make it healthier. This week, identify when you tend to snack and keep wholesome options on hand. Replace crisps with air-popped popcorn or nuts, and trade sugary sweets for naturally sweet treats like fresh fruit or a piece of dark chocolate. Pre-portion your snacks so you can grab a healthy option easily when hunger strikes. By the end of the week, aim to make your snacks largely consist of whole, minimally processed foods.

Week 4: Elevate Your Lunch

Now that your snacks are sorted, let's focus on lunch! Quick fixes like takeaways and ready meals can often be loaded with unhealthy ingredients. Upgrade your midday meal by incorporating whole foods. Instead of regular bread, opt for wholegrain options and pile on the veggies. Whip up salads with homemade dressings using olive oil and vinegar, no hidden sugars here. Lean proteins like grilled chicken or beans will keep you satisfied all afternoon. Start by preparing one healthier lunch each day and gradually extend it to the full week.

Week 5: Transform Your Dinner Plate

Let's shine a light on dinner! This week, follow the "half-plate rule": fill half your plate with colourful veggies, one-quarter with lean protein, and the last quarter with whole grains or starchy vegetables, like sweet potatoes. If you tend to grab processed dinners, try your hand at homemade meals. Roast vibrant veggies alongside grilled fish or try a delicious stir-fry packed with tofu and brown rice. Meal prepping will save you time and keep healthy choices within reach.

Week 6: Tame Your Condiments

It's time to take a good look at those condiments. Many shop bought sauces are sneaky sources of added sugars and unhealthy fats. Check the labels on ketchup or salad dressings. Swap out these processed choices for fantastic, wholesome alternatives. Consider using olive oil and lemon juice in place of dressing, or Greek yoghurt instead of mayo. By the end of the week, your meals will burst with fresh flavours and feel cleaner.

Week 7: Master Portion Control

With your meals and snacks on point, let's turn our attention to how much you eat. Even the healthiest foods can lead to weight gain if portions get out of hand. Use smaller plates and bowls to help keep portion sizes in check, and tune into your hunger signals. Try eating slowly and stop when you're satisfied, not stuffed. Measuring out grains and proteins can also keep you mindful of serving sizes. By the end of this week, you'll build a more balanced and intuitive approach to eating.

Remember to enjoy each small victory along the way! With each week, you'll feel more empowered and excited about your food choices.

The Power of Patience and Discipline

When embarking on a journey of meaningful transformation, patience and consistency are your companions. Whether you're aiming to revamp your diet, get moving with regular exercise, or kick unhealthy habits to the curb, remember this: lasting change unfolds gradually. In our fast-paced world, it's all too easy to feel impatient when results don't appear instantly. But just like a garden takes time to flourish, the best transformations blossom over time.

Discipline is the driving force that steers us through this transformative process. It's not about hitting perfection every single day; rather, it's about showing up and putting in the effort, even when motivation is lacking. Sure, motivation can be that initial spark, but it's discipline that keeps your fire burning. Think of discipline as a muscle: the more you use it, the stronger it becomes. It's the ability to push past those tempting excuses, whether that means resisting fast food after a long day or committing to a quick walk instead of skipping exercise altogether.

Let's take a closer look at an example that illustrates these principles beautifully: meet Sarah, a 35-year-old teacher determined to enhance her health and shed some weight. After years of battling unhealthy eating habits and low energy, she decided it was time for a change. Faced with the daunting task ahead. This time, however, she chose a different path, one paved with small, sustainable changes.

Sarah kick-started her journey with a single, simple habit: drinking more water. For two weeks, she focused on replacing sugary drinks with refreshing water and herbal teas. She wasn't perfect, there were days when fizzy drinks called to her, but overall, she remained consistent. Once drinking water became second nature, she added another layer to her journey by incorporating more vegetables into her meals, aiming for at least one serving at lunch and dinner. These small shifts snowballed over a few months. To her delight, Sarah began noticing a drop in junk food cravings and a surge in her energy levels.

Of course, the road wasn't always smooth. There were moments when Sarah felt as if her efforts were yielding no visible change, and the temptation to give up was strong. Yet, she reminded herself that true transformation takes time and that every effort counts. Armed with a journal, she started tracking her small victories, whether it was preparing a healthy lunch or completing a 20-minute workout. This not only kept her motivated but also reinforced her belief in her journey. By staying patient and committed, Sarah successfully lost 11kg over the course of a year, not through crash diets, but by building habits she could genuinely embrace for life.

Sarah's journey teaches us a vital lesson: even the smallest of consistent actions can lead to remarkable outcomes. Patience is key here. Change doesn't happen in a flash, and expecting instant results can lead to frustration. Instead, immerse yourself in the process, and trust that your efforts are laying a strong foundation for long-term success. Remember, progress is rarely a straight line; you will face setbacks and plateaus along the way. Embrace them as part of the journey, not the end.

Consistency is not about achieving perfection; it's about continuing to show up, often, even after setbacks. If you miss a workout or indulge in a treat, don't let it derail your entire progress. Instead, pick yourself up and get back at it the next day. One misstep doesn't undo all the hard work you've done; what matters is your response. Over time, those small, consistent actions will become ingrained habits, and the desired results will surely follow.

Discipline is the glue that harmonises patience and consistency. It propels you forward when motivation falters. While it's easy to feel excited at the start of a new venture, it's discipline that truly keeps you committed to your goals once the initial thrill fades. Establish clear intentions and follow through, even when it's inconvenient. If you vow to exercise three times a week, it's discipline that will push you to hit the gym on particularly busy days or motivate you to take that post-dinner stroll instead of collapsing on the couch. With practice, discipline becomes less of a chore and more of a natural part of your routine.

Moreover, discipline isn't about being hard on yourself; it's an expression of self-respect and care. By keeping your commitments, you're putting your health and well-being first. It's a gesture of self-love that boldly declares, "I'm worth the effort." Each time you honour your commitments, you boost your confidence and strengthen your belief in your ability to create positive change.

If you ever feel disheartened, remember that progress compounds over time. Picture a jar slowly filling with tiny drops of water, each one seems insignificant, yet collectively they lead to a full jar. Each healthy meal, every workout, and every day you stick to your plan contributes to your growth, even if immediate results aren't evident. Embrace the journey, trust the process, and watch as your transformation unfolds before your eyes.

Chapter 6: Exercise and Its Role in Health

Understanding how your body uses energy is crucial for mastering weight management and enhancing overall health. At the core of this energetic story are three key players: calories, metabolism, and exercise. When you break it down, it becomes much clearer. Think of calories as the energy your body runs on, metabolism as the engine that utilises that energy, and exercise as the tool that helps you burn off excess fuel. Let's dive deeper into this fascinating interplay.

First off, let's talk about calories. These little units of energy are found in every bite you take, fuelling everything your body does, from breathing and digesting food to exercising and even typing on your keyboard. Here's a fun fact: If you consume more calories than your body needs, it stores the extra as fat. On the flip side, when you eat less than you burn, your body taps into those fat reserves for energy, leading to weight loss.

Now, how exactly does your body use these calories? It primarily burns them in three ways. The first is through your Basal Metabolic Rate (BMR), the energy your body needs just to keep things running. Factors like age, gender, muscle mass, and genetics play a big role here. For example, if you're rocking a higher muscle mass, you're likely burning more calories at rest simply because muscle is a more demanding tissue than fat.

Next up is the Thermic Effect of Food (TEF). This is the energy your body expends to digest and process the food you eat. Interestingly, not all foods are created equal in this department. For instance, protein requires more energy to break down compared to fats or carbs. So, a protein-rich diet can provide a small boost to your calorie burn.

The third way your body burns calories is through physical activity, that's right, the good old movement! This encompasses everything from a sweat inducing gym session to the little things like cleaning your house. The beauty of physical activity is that it offers you control by stepping up your movement, you can ramp up your calorie expenditure.

Now, let's get to the heart of fat loss: creating a calorie deficit. This magical state occurs when you burn more calories than you consume. When your body doesn't have sufficient energy from food, it turns to stored fat for fuel. This is where exercise plays its starring role, helping you burn more calories and effectively enhance that deficit.

But how does exercise burn fat? Your body primarily relies on two fuel sources: carbohydrates and fat. When you engage in low-intensity activities, your body prefers fat for energy because it can break it down more gradually. As the intensity ramps up, your body shifts gears and starts to utilise more carbohydrates for quick energy. Regardless of the intensity, the total calories burned is what counts most for shedding fat.

Aerobic exercises, such as walking, running, or cycling, are fantastic for burning calories and fat. They get your heart racing and keep it elevated for longer periods, ramping up your cardio fitness and efficiency in using fat as fuel. For example, a 30-minute walk can burn around 150-200 calories, depending on your weight and pace. Stick with consistent aerobic exercise alongside a balanced diet, and you'll likely see notable fat loss over time.

Then there's strength training, which brings a unique twist to your fat-loss journey. While it might not burn as many calories during your workouts as cardio does, it's invaluable for building and maintaining muscle mass. And remember, more muscle means a higher resting metabolism, so you'll be burning more calories even when you're binge-watching your favourite show. Incorporating weightlifting or bodyweight exercises, like squats and push-ups, into your routine a few times a week can have a profound impact on your overall calorie burn.

Don't forget about the exciting "afterburn effect," also known as Excess Post-Exercise Oxygen Consumption (EPOC). After an intense workout, your body continues to burn calories at a higher rate while it recovers. This effect is even more noticeable with high-intensity workouts, like interval training or circuit training, where you alternate bursts of intense activity with short rest periods. These workouts are incredibly efficient for burning fat and ramping up your fitness in a fraction of the time.

Ultimately, understanding how calories, metabolism, and exercise work together empowers you to take charge of your health journey.

Cardio, Strength and Flexibility

By understanding the three main types of exercise, cardio, strength training and flexibility, you can craft a comprehensive fitness routine that perfectly aligns with your dietary goals. Each type brings its own unique flair to the table, and together, they create a recipe for success.

Let's dive into cardio, or aerobic exercise, which is all about getting your heart pumping and blood flowing. Picture yourself walking, running, cycling, swimming, or even busting a move on the dance floor. Cardio is your go-to for burning calories and boosting your cardiovascular health. When paired with a thoughtful calorie-controlled diet, regular cardio sessions help carve out the calorie deficit needed for effective fat loss.

But the benefits don't stop at calorie burning. Cardio workouts enhance your heart and lung function, ramping up your endurance and energy levels over time. Plus, it plays a vital role in regulating blood sugar and cholesterol levels, which is crucial for long term health. If you're just starting your fitness journey, low impact cardio options like walking or cycling are fantastic ways to dip your toes in without overwhelming your joints. As you get comfortable, you can gradually increase the intensity or duration to keep challenging yourself.

Next up is strength training, sometimes known as resistance training. This form of exercise focuses on building strength and endurance by targeting specific muscle groups. It could involve lifting weights, using resistance bands, or simply performing bodyweight exercises like squats, press ups, and planks. While cardio works wonders for burning calories during your workouts, strength training offers a powerful edge: it helps you build and maintain lean muscle mass. Remember, muscle is a calorie-burning machine, even when you're resting! By boosting your muscle mass, you supercharge your basal metabolic rate (BMR), meaning you'll burn more calories throughout the day, even while relaxing.

Furthermore, strength training works harmoniously with dietary changes to improve your body composition. As you create a calorie deficit and shed pounds, strength training ensures that the weight you lose primarily comes from fat instead of muscle. This is especially important for maintaining your strength and functionality as the years go by. There's no need for fancy weights or equipment, simple, effective moves like lunges, press-ups, and resistance band rows can be done right at home. For maximum benefits, aim to incorporate strength training into your routine two to three times a week, targeting all major muscle groups.

Now, don't overlook the power of flexibility training, it's just as crucial as cardio and strength work. These exercises are designed to enhance your range of motion, alleviate muscle stiffness, and boost overall mobility. Think stretching, yoga, and Pilates! Flexibility training not only helps prevent injuries but also improves posture and promotes a sense of relaxation. It's particularly beneficial when making dietary changes, as it can relieve muscle soreness caused by increased activity and speed up your recovery after workouts.

Flexibility exercises also play a supporting role in your fitness and diet goals by enhancing your movement patterns. For example, improved flexibility in your hips and hamstrings makes strength exercises like squats and deadlifts safer and more effective. Plus, activities like yoga often blend mindfulness and breathing techniques, helping to reduce stress and reduce emotional eating. Even a brief daily stretching routine or a weekly yoga session can significantly impact how your body feels and performs.

Combining cardio, strength training, and flexibility exercises creates a well-rounded fitness routine that complements your dietary adjustments and supports a healthier you. Here's the magic: cardio helps burn calories and boost heart health; strength training builds muscle and revs up your metabolism; and flexibility work ensures you stay injury-free and move with ease. Together, these elements work in harmony to amplify the benefits of a nutritious diet.

So, if your goal is weight loss, think of cardio as your ally in creating that calorie deficit. Meanwhile, strength training ensures that the weight you shed is primarily fat, not muscle. And don't forget about flexibility exercises, they help you recover faster and prevent injuries, making it easier to stick to your routine. If your aim is to enhance overall health and energy levels, these exercises complement each other beautifully, supporting your cardiovascular system, strengthening your muscles, and improving your mobility.

Exercises You Can Start With

Starting an exercise routine might seem daunting, but it doesn't have to be. With a few simple and approachable steps, you can dive into physical activity and gradually build strength, endurance, and flexibility. This plan is all about helping you create a fun and balanced fitness journey that includes cardio, strength training, and flexibility exercises, all designed specifically for beginners and tailored for gradual progress. By committing to exercise three to five days a week and mixing up these activities, you'll forge a routine that's not only effective but also sustainable and enjoyable.

Let's kick things off with cardio, which is an excellent way to get your heart pumping and your body moving! Walking is one of the simplest and most rewarding options for beginners. Start with a 20-minute walk at a pace that leaves you pleasantly out of breath yet still able to chat. If you can't get outside, no worries, jump on a treadmill or march in place at home! As you get comfortable, challenge yourself by gradually increasing your duration or throwing in some short bursts of faster walking or light jogging. And remember, cycling or beginner dance workouts are fantastic alternatives if that's more your style. The key is to find something you enjoy, consistency is key!

Next up is strength training, a fantastic way to build muscle, improve posture, and increase your metabolism. This beginner-friendly strength circuit relies on simple bodyweight exercises, no fancy equipment required. Start with two rounds of exercises, aiming for 10-12 repetitions, and give yourself 30-60 seconds of rest in between. Think bodyweight squats, wall push-ups, glute bridges, and standing overhead reaches, these moves target all the major muscle groups without straining your joints. As you progress, you can add more rounds, ramp up your repetitions, or even grab light weights like water bottles or cans for a little extra challenge!

And don't forget about flexibility exercises. They're crucial for improving your range of motion. A simple stretching routine can include nurturing movements like the cat-cow stretch, hamstring stretches, seated side stretches, and child's pose. Hold each stretch for 15-20 seconds to start, and as you become more flexible, feel free to extend that time. If you're looking for even more relaxation, beginner yoga videos can be a wonderful addition.

To make sure this plan fits seamlessly into your life, start slow and really listen to your body. Remember, it's perfectly fine to do less and stay consistent, this is far better than overdoing it and risking injury. Keep track of your progress by jotting down your workouts and how you feel afterwards. This not only helps you stay motivated but also highlights just how far you've come. And if life gets hectic? No sweat, even a 10-minute workout can still make a difference.

This holistic approach to exercise combines cardio for calorie burning and endurance, strength training for muscle building and a metabolic boost, and flexibility exercises to enhance mobility and support recovery. By starting with manageable steps and gradually expanding your routine, you're laying a solid foundation for long-term health and fitness. Stick with it, and you'll notice a wonderful transformation in your energy levels, strength, and overall well-being.

Chapter 7: Setting Goals and Tracking Progress

Setting your sights on success in health and fitness starts with a powerful yet simple practice: writing down your goals. Whether it's shedding a few pounds, building muscle, or simply feeling better day to day, having clear goals acts as your compass on the journey ahead. It's not just about dreaming; it's about transforming those dreams into a concrete plan that drives you. When your goals are written down, they become tangible targets that energise and inspire you. So, let's explore why this practice is so transformative and how you can harness its power.

The first step in goal setting is to connect with what truly matters to you. Take a moment to reflect on why you want to make a change. Is it to boost your confidence, increase your energy, or enhance your long-term health? Identifying your "why" is crucial; it acts as your anchor when motivation decreases. Once you've clarified your purpose, it's time to get specific. Instead of vague aspirations like "I want to lose weight," aim for a clearer target: "I want to lose 10 pounds in the next three months." Specific goals make your aspirations feel achievable and allow you to track your progress effectively.

Think about the SMART criteria when crafting your goals: Specific, Measurable, Achievable, Relevant, and Time-bound. For instance, instead of just wanting to get fit, reframe it as, "I will jog for 20 minutes three times a week for the next month." This is specific (jogging), measurable (20 minutes, three times a week), achievable (great for a beginner), relevant (focused on fitness), and time-bound (next month). SMART goals help keep you grounded while providing clear milestones to celebrate along the way.

Now, let's talk about strategy! Breaking your larger goals into smaller, manageable steps can make the journey feel less daunting. If your aim is to lose 10kg, take it one step at a time, start with a goal of losing 1kg. Celebrate each small victory as you progress; these wins can boost your confidence and keep the momentum rolling. Similarly, if your dream is to run a 5K, begin with short jogging intervals and gradually extend your distance. Focusing on incremental progress not only provides a sense of accomplishment but also fuels your motivation.

Holding yourself accountable through written documentation can significantly enhance your goal-setting process. Consider keeping a journal, planner, or using a digital app to track your progress. For example, if enhancing your diet is your goal, jot down your meals each day and note any positive changes, like incorporating more vegetables or cutting back on sugary snacks. If fitness is the focus, record details about your workouts: types of exercise, duration, and how you felt afterwards. Seeing your progress on paper can be a powerful motivator and help you remain consistent.

Visualisation is a game-changer in achieving your goals. When you write them down, take a moment to imagine the pure joy of achieving them. Envision yourself crossing that race finish line or slipping into that outfit you love. This mental imagery not only reinforces your commitment but also serves as a reminder of why these goals mean so much to you. Adding a visual component, such as a vision board or inspiring images, can make the process even more thrilling.

Don't forget to balance both short-term and long-term goals. Short-term wins, like drinking more water daily or committing to workouts three times a week, keep your spirits high while building solid habits. Meanwhile, long-term aspirations, such as reaching a healthy weight or training for a marathon, keep your eyes on the prize. This balance between immediate achievements and overarching dreams ensures you remain motivated today while looking ahead to the bigger picture.

Embrace flexibility in your journey toward your goals. Life can throw curveballs, so when setbacks occur, view them as opportunities to adjust your approach rather than failures. Did you miss a week of workouts because of unexpected events? No worries, simply pick up where you left off without any guilt. Regularly revisiting your written goals can ground you and remind you of how far you've come, even when the path isn't perfectly smooth.

Sharing your goals with someone supportive can provide an extra layer of motivation and accountability. Telling a friend or family member about your plans can give you that necessary boost, they may even want to join you on your fitness journey! Having someone cheering you on or checking in periodically makes the process feel more enjoyable and less isolating.

Lastly, take the time to celebrate every little achievement along the way. Whether you finished a week of consistent workouts, reached a gym milestone, or simply felt more energetic, recognising these successes reinforces all the hard work you've invested. Write down these victories and take pride in your progress.

Chapter 8: The Power of Sleep and Its Impact on Health

Sleep is often the unsung hero of health and wellness discussions, yet it holds a mighty power over our metabolism, hunger regulation, and energy levels. A good night's sleep goes far beyond mere rest; it's a crucial time when our bodies recover, balance hormones, and prepare us for the day ahead. Without proper sleep, even the most well-planned diet and exercise regime can feel like pushing a boulder uphill. Let's dive into the ways sleep influences our metabolism, hunger hormones, and energy levels, and discover why prioritising quality rest is essential for reaching your health goals.

Think of sleep as a key player in the metabolism game. Your metabolism is the process that transforms food into energy, and it never actually takes a break, even while you sleep! When we sleep, our bodies engage in vital repair work, hormone regulation, and energy conservation. These processes are fundamental for maintaining a healthy metabolic rate, the rate at which your body burns calories when at rest. But skimping on sleep can slow down your metabolism, making it tougher to lose weight or keep it off. Studies show that lack of sleep can lead to diminished insulin sensitivity, altering how your body processes sugar and increasing your risk of weight gain and metabolic issues, including type 2 diabetes.

One of the most important connections between sleep and metabolism involves hormones, particularly ghrelin and leptin. Ghrelin, known as the "hunger hormone," sends the signal to your brain that it's time to eat, while leptin, the "fullness hormone," tells your brain you've had enough. When you don't get enough sleep, these hormones become imbalanced, ghrelin levels spike, and leptin levels dip. This imbalance can leave you feeling hungrier than usual, even if your body doesn't actually require more calories. It's no wonder that after a night of tossing and turning, we crave those high-calorie snacks that are sugary or fatty!

Sleep also impacts cortisol, the stress hormone. When you're deprived of sleep, cortisol levels rise, which can have several adverse effects on your metabolism. Elevated cortisol is linked to increased cravings, especially for comforting, high-sugar, and high-fat foods. It can also promote the storage of fat, particularly around the waist, making weight loss feel like a daunting task. Plus, elevated cortisol can disrupt insulin function, leading to blood sugar issues and reduced energy levels.

Now, let's not underestimate the importance of sleep on our energy levels. Quality sleep is essential for rejuvenating both our physical and mental energy. During deep sleep, our bodies repair muscles and tissues, boost our immune system, and consolidate memories. Without sufficient sleep, these restorative processes are compromised, leaving you tired and less motivated to stay active. This can create a vicious cycle: low energy gets in the way of maintaining a healthy lifestyle, which in turn affects sleep quality.

It's not just the amount of sleep that counts; the quality is equally critical. Tossing and turning, waking up frequently, or failing to delve into deep or REM sleep can wreak havoc on metabolism and hormone levels, just like sleep deprivation can. Factors such as stress, excessive screen time before bed, and irregular sleep schedules can disrupt your ability to enjoy restful sleep. That's why fostering healthy sleep habits, like establishing a regular sleep routine and creating a calming bedtime environment is so crucial.

To truly harness the benefits of sleep for your metabolism, hunger hormones, and energy, aim for 8 hours of quality sleep each night. Consistency is essential: heading to bed and rising at the same time every day will help regulate your body's internal clock, or circadian rhythm. Reducing caffeine and alcohol intake, especially later in the day, can significantly enhance your sleep quality as well. Creating a sleep friendly haven, think cool, dark, and quiet can make falling asleep and staying asleep a breeze.

In conclusion, sleep is a fundamental pillar of health that directly impacts metabolism, hunger hormones, and energy levels. Insufficient sleep hampers your body's ability to regulate hunger and fullness, leading to increased cravings and potential weight gain. Lack of quality rest disrupts hormone balance, slows metabolism, and drains energy, making it more challenging to stay active and adhere to a healthy lifestyle. By prioritising quality sleep, you take one of the most effective steps to bolster your overall well-being and achieve your health aspirations. By understanding the transformative role sleep plays in your body's processes, you can start to prioritise it and enjoy the multitude of benefits that come from better rest.

Improving Your Sleep

One of the best ways to improve your sleep is to establish a bedtime routine. Think of it as giving your body a reliable schedule it can count on. Going to bed and waking up at the same time every day helps get your internal clock, known as the circadian rhythm, into gear. When your body anticipates sleep, it becomes easier to drift off and wake up feeling refreshed. Choose a bedtime and wake-up time that allows for 7-9 hours of sleep, and stick with it, even on weekends! It might take a couple of weeks for your body to adjust, but trust me, the payoff in sleep quality will be well worth it.

Let's talk about those screens. The blue light emitted by your phone, tablet, or television can throw a spanner in the works when it comes to melatonin production, the hormone responsible for regulating sleep. To give your brain the chance to wind down, try turning off screens at least an hour before bed. If you can't resist scrolling through your feed, consider some blue light-blocking glasses or use night mode on your devices. Instead of screen time, indulge in calming activities like reading a book, journaling, or listening to soothing music to ease into your evening.

A relaxing bedtime routine can be a game changer. Engage in simple, enjoyable activities to signal to your body that it's time to wind down. Maybe that means enjoying a warm bath, practising deep breathing, or giving meditation a try. Consider incorporating aromatherapy with lavender or chamomile essential oils to create a peaceful atmosphere in your bedroom. The aim is to transition from the busyness of your day into a state of calm, making it easier to relax and fall asleep.

Don't underestimate the power of your sleep environment! Your bedroom should be a sanctuary for rest, cool, dark, and quiet. Cooler rooms can help you achieve deeper sleep. Blackout curtains or an eye mask can block out disruptive light, and earplugs or a white noise machine can help mask outside noise. Also, try to reserve your bed strictly for sleep, so your brain associates it with rest rather than work or entertainment.

What you eat and drink, and when you exercise can greatly influence your sleep quality. Avoid caffeine and heavy meals close to bedtime, as these can make it difficult to fall asleep. And while a glass of wine might help you feel sleepy initially, it can interfere with the deeper, restorative stages of sleep, so it's wise to limit alcohol in the evening. On the flip side, regular exercise can significantly enhance your sleep quality; just aim to do it earlier in the day so you aren't too energised when it's time to sleep.

Stress and anxiety can create a whirlwind of thoughts that make it nearly impossible to relax at night. Incorporating stress-reducing practices like mindfulness meditation, progressive muscle relaxation, or gratitude journaling into your daily routine can work wonders. If you find yourself lying awake with racing thoughts, jot them down in a journal to clear your head and reassure yourself you can tackle them tomorrow.

Don't forget to listen to your body! Trying to force sleep can lead to frustration and anxiety. If you can't fall asleep after 20 minutes, get up and do something calm and non-stimulating until you feel drowsy. This practice helps keep your bed associated with rest and not wakefulness.

Improving sleep quality isn't just about making a few changes overnight; it's about creating a supportive blend of habits, a tranquil environment, and proactive stress management. With a consistent bedtime routine, minimised screen time, a comfortable sleep space, and attention to your lifestyle choices, you'll be setting the stage for deep, rejuvenating sleep. Patience is key, better sleep doesn't happen right away. However, the effort you put in is truly worth it, as quality sleep lays the foundation for a healthier, more vibrant life.

Lastly, for anyone on a journey to shed pounds or boost their health, one crucial element often gets overlooked: mental clarity. When it comes to making wise choices, focus and discipline are essential, and not getting enough sleep can throw a wrench in those gears. Research shows that sleep deprivation disrupts the prefrontal cortex, the part of your brain that handles decision making and self-control. This can make it all too easy to give in to cravings for sugary snacks or skip that workout, even when you know deep down what's best for your long-term goals.

But sleep does far more than help you resist temptations. It's also a game changer for regulating your emotions. A good night's sleep reduces stress and anxiety, which are often the culprits behind emotional eating and other unhealthy habits. When you're well rested, your productivity soars and your mood improves allowing you to tackle daily challenges with renewed energy. You'll find it easier to stay motivated and maintain a positive outlook, creating the perfect environment for pursuing your health and fitness objectives with enthusiasm.

Over time, the benefits of a good night's sleep snowball. Better decision-making, increased energy, and improved emotional resilience work together to fuel your progress in weight loss and overall wellness.

Prioritising sleep is more than just an easy way to feel rested; it's a fundamental building block for both physical and mental health. Quality sleep helps regulate hunger hormones, boost metabolism, and energise you making it simpler to lose weight and embrace healthy habits. Plus, it sharpens your mental clarity, focus, and emotional stability, equipping you with the tools to stay on track with your goals. So, if you want to unlock your mind and body's full potential for leading a healthier, more balanced life, make sleep a priority!

Chapter 9: The Benefits of Healthy Fasting Habits

Fasting and dieting often get lumped together, but they're worlds apart when it comes to their methods and effects on our health. Understanding these distinctions can empower you to make smarter choices for your well-being. Healthy fasting shines as a sustainable approach to enhancing metabolic health, regulating appetites, and shedding unwanted pounds, while extreme dieting can lead to harmful habits, nutritional gaps, and greater risks to both physical and mental health. Let's dive into the intriguing differences between these two pathways.

Imagine healthy fasting as a structured rhythm to your meals, emphasising when you eat rather than obsessing over every bite. Popular methods like the 16:8 (fast for 16 hours, eat for 8) and the 5:2 (normal meals for five days, significantly reduced calories on two non-consecutive days) offer flexibility and balance. The beauty of healthy fasting lies in granting your body breaks from constant digestion, allowing it to focus on vital tasks like cellular repair and hormonal balance. During these fasting windows, your body switches from burning sugar to tapping into fat reserves, which can contribute to weight loss and better metabolic health.

One of the most promising aspects of healthy fasting is its power to enhance your body's energy management capabilities. Research shows that fasting can boost insulin sensitivity, lower inflammation, and stabilise blood sugar levels, all essential factors in preventing chronic issues like diabetes and heart disease. It's not about depriving yourself; it's about being intentional with your eating schedule while savouring a nutrient-rich diet during your meals, making it a sustainable lifestyle choice tailored to your personal preferences.

Now, let's contrast that with extreme diets. These often come loaded with strict rules that may ban whole food groups or slash calorie intake to shocking levels. Think juice cleanses or bizarre detox diets. Sure, they might promise rapid weight loss, but at what cost? Such diets frequently rob your body of essential nutrients, lead to muscle loss, and can harm your overall health. They can also foster a toxic relationship with food, where pleasure turns to stress, guilt, or obsession. The cycle of yo-yo dieting often follows, where you lose weight only to regain it, frustrate yourself, and start over again.

One major flaw of extreme diets is their ability to lead your body astray in terms of nutrition. For instance, eliminating carbs altogether can cause fatigue, brain fog, and digestive issues, as carbohydrates are your body's primary energy source. And if you opt for a drastically low-calorie regimen, your metabolism may slow down as your body enters "starvation mode," making weight loss even more challenging over time. Essential vitamins, minerals, and protein for muscle repair and immune function could also be out of reach due to severe restrictions.

Hormones play a critical role in distinguishing healthy fasting from extreme dieting. Healthy fasting helps your body maintain a natural balance of hormones like insulin, ghrelin (the hunger hormone), and leptin (the fullness hormone). Meanwhile, extreme dieting often throws those signals into chaos, spiking ghrelin levels and leaving you perpetually hungry. This hormonal turmoil can set you on a dangerous path towards binge eating, while healthy fasting fosters hormonal stability as your system learns to adapt to a consistent eating and fasting pattern.

Mental health presents another significant divergence. Healthy fasting can cultivate a sense of control, encouraging you to plan meals mindfully and connect with your body's hunger signals. It embraces the joy of eating without the harsh restrictions typical of extreme diets, which can spark feelings of deprivation and frustration. This negativity spiral can lead to self-criticism and unhealthy eating behaviours.

Ultimately, sustainability stands out as the core difference. Healthy fasting is a lifestyle choice designed to seamlessly integrate into your daily life; it doesn't compel you to give up your favourite foods or adhere to complex rules. In contrast, extreme diets are often marketed as quick fixes with grand promises, yet their restrictive nature makes them difficult to sustain. When the diet ends, many individuals find themselves drawn back to old habits, leading to that frustrating pattern we all wish to escape.

Common Fasting Methods

One of the most widely practiced forms of fasting is intermittent fasting. This method involves cycling between periods of eating and fasting, focusing more on when you eat rather than what you eat. Within intermittent fasting, there are several popular patterns. One of the simplest is the 16:8 method, where you fast for 16 hours each day and eat during an 8-hour window. For example, if you finish dinner at 7 p.m. you wouldn't eat again until 11 a.m. the next day. This approach works well for many people because the fasting period includes sleep, making it easier to stick to.

Another common form of intermittent fasting is the 5:2 method, where you eat normally for five days of the week and reduce your calorie intake significantly (typically to 500-600 calories) on two non-consecutive days. This approach provides the flexibility of eating normally most days while still reaping the benefits of fasting. Some people prefer alternate day fasting, where they alternate between a day of normal eating and a day of fasting or very low-calorie intake.

Time-restricted eating is a specific type of intermittent fasting that focuses on limiting food intake to a certain number of hours each day. For instance, someone might choose to eat only between 10 a.m. and 6 p.m., leaving a 14-hour fasting window. This method aligns with the body's natural circadian rhythm, which is the internal clock that regulates many physiological processes, including digestion. By eating during daylight hours and fasting overnight, time-restricted eating supports optimal metabolic function.

The benefits of these fasting methods extend beyond weight loss. One of the primary advantages is improved metabolic health. During fasting periods, the body shifts from using sugar as its primary energy source to burning stored fat for fuel. This metabolic switch, known as ketosis, can help reduce body fat and support weight loss. Additionally, fasting improves insulin sensitivity, making it easier for the body to regulate blood sugar levels and reducing the risk of developing type 2 diabetes.

Fasting also promotes cellular repair and regeneration. During fasting periods, the body initiates a process in which damaged cells and cellular components are broken down and recycled. This natural "clean-up" process helps remove toxins, repair cellular damage, and reduce inflammation. Autophagy is thought to play a role in preventing chronic diseases, such as heart disease and neurodegenerative disorders, by promoting overall cellular health.

For those seeking improved energy levels and focus, fasting can also help by stabilising blood sugar and avoiding the energy crashes associated with frequent snacking or high-carb meals. Many people report feeling more alert and productive during fasting periods, as the body operates more efficiently when not constantly digesting food. This heightened focus can be especially beneficial for individuals with demanding schedules or mental tasks.

It's important to note that fasting is not a one-size-fits-all approach. Different methods work for different people, and it's essential to choose a fasting pattern that aligns with your lifestyle, preferences, and health goals. For example, someone with a busy morning schedule might find the 16:8 method convenient because they can skip breakfast and start eating later in the day. On the other hand, someone who enjoys eating breakfast may prefer the 5:2 method, as it allows for more flexibility during the week.

When practicing fasting, it's crucial to focus on the quality of your diet during eating periods. Fasting is not a license to overeat or indulge in unhealthy foods, it works best when paired with a balanced, nutrient-rich diet. Include plenty of whole foods, such as lean proteins, healthy fats, whole grains, fruits, and vegetables, to ensure your body gets the nutrients it needs. Staying hydrated is equally important, especially during fasting periods, as water helps maintain energy and supports the body's natural detoxification processes.

It's also worth noting that fasting may not be suitable for everyone. Pregnant or breastfeeding individuals, people with certain medical conditions, or those with a history of disordered eating should consult a healthcare professional before attempting any fasting regimen. Listening to your body is key, if fasting causes significant discomfort or interferes with your well-being, it may not be the right approach for you.

Intermittent fasting and time-restricted eating offer flexible and effective ways to improve health, manage weight, and boost overall well-being. These methods work by giving the body regular breaks from digestion, promoting fat metabolism, enhancing cellular repair, and supporting brain health. By choosing a fasting pattern that suits your lifestyle and pairing it with a nutritious diet, you can enjoy the many benefits of these practices in a sustainable and enjoyable way. As with any health strategy, consistency and mindfulness are key to long-term success!

Chapter 10: Managing Stress for Better Health

Stress hormones, especially cortisol, have a significant impact on how our bodies manage weight. By exploring how cortisol functions, what triggers its release during stressful times, and its role in weight gain, we can find effective strategies to manage stress and achieve our health goals. While cortisol is crucial for our survival, it can produce unwanted effects on weight and metabolism when stress becomes a constant companion.

Cortisol is produced by our adrenal glands whenever we face stress. It's a key player in the body's "fight or flight" response, a survival mechanism designed to help us tackle immediate threats. When something stressful arises, a looming deadline, a heated argument, or even physical danger, our brains signal the adrenal glands to unleash cortisol. This hormone elevates glucose levels in our bloodstream, providing the body with a quick energy boost while also sidelining non-essential functions like digestion and reproduction, allowing us to stay laser-focused on the challenge at hand.

In short bursts, cortisol is a powerhouse. It keeps us alert, energised, and ready to tackle life's hurdles. However, the real trouble begins when stress becomes chronic, leading to persistently high cortisol levels. Chronic stress can stem from a variety of sources: work pressures, financial troubles, or challenging relationships. When cortisol lingers at elevated levels, it starts to create a cascade of effects that encourage weight gain and other health complications.

One of the primary culprits in weight gain linked to cortisol is its tendency to increase appetite. Elevated levels of cortisol trigger the release of ghrelin, known as the "hunger hormone." Ghrelin sparks cravings for high-calorie comfort foods that are often sugary and fatty. Who hasn't reached for biscuits, crisps, or ice cream in a stressful moment? While these treats offer a sweet escape, they contribute to excess calorie consumption, making it challenging to maintain a healthy weight.

Moreover, cortisol signals our bodies to store fat, particularly around the belly. This happens because high cortisol levels suggest to our bodies that it's time to conserve energy for potential future threats. Unfortunately, this translates to increased visceral fat, which wraps around vital organs like the liver and intestines. Visceral fat is notoriously stubborn and harmful, linked to a heightened risk of heart disease, diabetes, and other metabolic issues.

Cortisol's influence extends to blood sugar regulation as well. When cortisol spikes, it raises blood glucose levels, prompting the pancreas to release insulin to restore balance. However, this cycle can become problematic. If cortisol remains high over time, it may lead to insulin resistance, where the cells in our body become less responsive to insulin. This condition complicates blood sugar management and increases the likelihood of weight gain, especially around the waist. It's a vicious cycle, stress elevates cortisol, disrupts blood sugar levels, leading to more stress and further cortisol release.

Additionally, chronic stress and high cortisol can slow our metabolism. Research indicates that prolonged exposure to heightened cortisol may reduce our metabolic rate, making it harder to burn calories even if our eating habits stay the same. To make matters worse, cortisol can break down muscle for immediate energy during stressful times, leading to reduced muscle mass. Since muscle tissue burns more calories at rest than fat, losing muscle makes maintaining or shedding weight even more difficult.

Beyond the physical, cortisol can affect our emotional and behavioural reactions to stress. Many individuals resort to food for comfort during stressful periods, a behaviour known as emotional eating. While it might provide a momentary sense of relief, this often results in overeating and added weight over time. To complicate things further, elevated cortisol levels can disrupt sleep patterns, creating a cycle that exacerbates the weight gain issue.

It's essential to balance our diets alongside stress management. Incorporating foods rich in antioxidants, fruits and vegetables can help combat inflammation triggered by stress. By understanding the powerful connection between stress hormones and weight, we can take actionable steps toward a healthier, more balanced life.

Stress Management Techniques

Managing stress is essential for maintaining a healthy and balanced life, and it's something we all need to prioritise. Chronic stress doesn't just take a toll on your mental well-being; it can seriously affect your physical health too. Thankfully, there are effective techniques to help you tame that stress monster. By incorporating practices like mindfulness, deep breathing, and exercise into your daily routine, you can enhance your emotional resilience and tackle life's challenges with a calmer approach. Let's dive into these methods and discover how they can transform your stress response and lead you to a more peaceful lifestyle.

Mindfulness

Imagine being able to focus entirely on the present moment, free of judgement and distractions. This is the essence of mindfulness, a powerful tool for stress management. When you're feeling overwhelmed, taking just a few minutes to check in with your breath, notice your body's sensations, and observe your thoughts can help you regain control and clarity. Mindfulness is proven to reduce the production of stress hormones like cortisol, leading to better emotional regulation.

Don't worry if you're not an expert in meditation; you can easily weave mindfulness into your day. Consider mindful eating, where you savour every bite of your meal, or mindful walking, where you tune into the rhythm of your steps and the sounds of the world around you. If you're new to mindfulness, apps like Headspace and Calm are great companions for guided meditations. With regular practice, you'll find a sense of calm that permeates every corner of your life.

Deep Breathing

When stress hits, our breathing often becomes quick and shallow, sending our bodies into a state of alert. However, deep breathing can effortlessly turn this around by activating your parasympathetic nervous system, ushering in relaxation. One popular technique is deep breathing, where you inhale deeply through your nose, letting your belly expand, and then exhale slowly through your mouth.

Try the 4-7-8 technique: inhale through your nose for four counts, hold for seven, and slowly exhale through your mouth for eight counts. Repeat this a few times, and you'll likely feel a wave of calm wash over you. What's great is that you can practise deep breathing wherever you are, sitting at your desk, lying in bed, or sneaking in a moment during a busy day. It's quick, effective, and requires nothing more than your breath.

Exercise

Let's not forget one of the most exhilarating ways to manage stress, movement! Exercise is a fantastic stress reliever that reduces cortisol levels while flooding your body with feel-good endorphins. Regular physical activity doesn't just lift your mood; it also enhances sleep quality and boosts your energy levels, helping you face stress head-on. Whether you enjoy walking, jogging, swimming, or cycling, these activities can provide both physical release and mental clarity.

For those who love a more structured approach, yoga and pilates brilliantly blend movement, mindfulness, and controlled breathing. Poses like Child's Pose or Cat-Cow Stretch are wonderfully calming and can be done at home or in a studio. Plus, if you thrive on social interaction, joining a group class can create a sense of community, reducing feelings of isolation and stress.

Hobbies

Don't underestimate the value of doing what you love! Engaging in creative activities such as painting, gardening, or playing an instrument can be incredibly therapeutic. Spending time in nature is also a superb stress reliever, whether you're strolling through a park, hiking in the woods, or simply soaking up the sounds of the outdoors. Nature has a magical way of lowering stress levels and boosting your mood.

Social Support

Building a network of support is crucial for managing stress. Sharing your worries with a trusted friend, family member, or therapist can significantly ease your burden. Opening up not only brings relief but also offers perspective, making you feel less alone during tough times. If you're hesitant to express your feelings, consider joining a support group or online community where you can connect with others facing similar challenges.

Reduce Stress for a Healthier Lifestyle

Reducing stress is one of the most transformative shifts you can make for a healthier lifestyle, and it's time we give it the attention it truly deserves! Chronic stress isn't just a minor annoyance in our busy lives; it's a serious adversary that impacts our mental clarity and wreaks havoc on our bodies. When stress is left unmanaged, it can lead us down a path of unhealthy choices, hormonal chaos, and long-term health issues. But here's the good news: by actively managing and reducing stress, we can establish a solid foundation for vibrant physical health, emotional strength, and a more fulfilling approach to life.

On an emotional level, managing stress helps you foster a more positive outlook and greater resilience. Constant stress can lead to a whirlpool of anxiety, irritability, and burnout, making it tough to stay motivated and engaged in healthy living. However, when you find effective ways to manage stress, you're better equipped to tackle life's challenges head-on. This emotional stability allows you to pursue your goals, whether it's a healthier diet, regular exercise, or nurturing meaningful connections with confidence and purpose.

Moreover, reducing stress nurtures stronger social connections, which are vital for a healthy lifestyle. High stress often pushes us into withdrawal, straining relationships when we need support the most. When we manage stress, we communicate better and enjoy quality time with our loved ones. Remember, social support acts as a powerful buffer against stress, creating a positive loop that enhances mood and lowers tension.

Finally, reducing stress encourages a holistic approach to health, harmonising body and mind. When life's pressures diminish, you're more in tune with what your body truly needs like nourishing food, physical activity, and moments of self-care. Practices such as mindfulness and meditation boost self-awareness, helping you spot and tackle unhealthy habits before they spiral out of control.

Emphasising stress reduction is essential for achieving a healthier lifestyle. By mastering your stress, you'll enhance decision-making skills, balance hormones, improve sleep quality, protect your heart, and cultivate emotional resilience.

These benefits create a powerful ripple effect, making it easier to sustain healthy habits and accomplish your long-term wellness goals. Whether through relaxing mindfulness techniques, engaging in physical activities, or simply dedicating time to your favourite hobbies, prioritising stress reduction can work wonders for both your physical and mental well-being empowering you to live a more balanced and enjoyable life!

Chapter 11: Supplements and Nutrient Essentials

A balanced diet is a cornerstone of a vibrant and healthy lifestyle. It's not just about eating; it's about fuelling your body with essential nutrients that keep your energy levels up and your mind sharp. When our diets lack balance, we risk facing nutrient deficiencies that can lead to a range of physical and mental health concerns. By understanding the crucial role of a balanced diet, you can make empowering choices for your well-being.

So, what does a balanced diet look like? It's all about the right proportions of macronutrients, carbohydrates, proteins, and fats as well as micronutrients, which include vitamins and minerals. Each of these nutrients plays a vital part in supporting the body's myriad functions. Carbohydrates are your body's primary energy source, providing the fuel you need for everything from a morning run to a brainstorming session at work. Choosing complex carbohydrates like whole grains, vegetables, and legumes helps deliver a steady supply of energy, avoiding those annoying spikes and crashes associated with refined sugars.

Next up is protein, the building block of your body! Think of it as the essential component for muscle repair, enzyme production, and a robust immune system. Lean proteins, such as chicken, fish, tofu, and beans, offer these benefits without adding excessive saturated fats to your diet. And let's not forget about healthy fats! Foods like avocados, nuts, seeds, and olive oil are not just tasty; they're crucial for brain health, hormone production, and helping your body absorb vital nutrients.

While we often focus on macronutrients, let's not overlook micronutrients. Vitamins such as A, C, D, E, and the B-complex group are key players in ensuring your immune system is strong, your energy levels are high, and your skin and eyes stay healthy.

Minerals like calcium, magnesium, potassium, and iron are equally important, they contribute to everything from bone strength to muscle function and oxygen transport throughout your body.

One of the standout benefits of maintaining a balanced diet is its power to reduce the risk of chronic diseases. Diets abundant in fruits, vegetables, whole grains, lean proteins, and healthy fats are linked to a lower likelihood of heart disease, diabetes, and certain cancers. For instance, the fibre found in fruits and vegetables helps regulate blood sugar levels and lower cholesterol. Meanwhile, antioxidants protect your body from oxidative stress, a precursor to various diseases. Plus, a nutrient-rich diet is vital for mental health, supplying your brain with what it needs to produce mood-regulating neurotransmitters like serotonin and dopamine.

Conversely, an unbalanced diet can lead to frustrating nutrient deficiencies. These happen when your body doesn't get enough of a specific vitamin or mineral to function optimally. Take iron deficiency, for example. It can lead to anaemia, which may leave you feeling fatigued and weak, as your body struggles to produce enough haemoglobin, the protein that carries oxygen in your blood. Including iron-rich foods like lean meats, spinach, lentils, and fortified cereals can prevent this pesky issue.

Another common culprit is vitamin D, often dubbed the "sunshine vitamin" because your body produces it in sunlight. This vitamin is essential for bone health, immune function, and even mood stability. A deficiency can often result in an increased vulnerability to fractures, not to mention feelings of depression. While basking in the sun is great, you can also find vitamin D in fatty fish, egg yolks, and fortified dairy products, particularly if you live in areas with limited sunlight.

Calcium deficiency is a significant concern, especially for children, teens, and older adults. Calcium is vital for maintaining strong bones and teeth while also supporting muscle function and nerve signalling. Insufficient calcium can lead to weakened bones and raise the risk of osteoporosis as we age. Incorporate dairy products, leafy greens, and fortified plant-based milks into your meals to keep those bones strong!

Vitamin B12 deficiency, which is particularly prevalent among vegetarians and older adults. This crucial vitamin supports red blood cell formation, DNA synthesis, and nerve health. A shortage can result in fatigue. Since B12 is predominantly found in animal products, those following a plant-based diet may require fortified foods or supplements.

Lastly, for individuals who enjoy a limited range of foods, be aware of the risk of magnesium deficiency. This essential mineral is involved in over 300 biochemical processes, playing a key role in energy production, muscle contractions, and nerve function. Signs of deficiency include muscle cramps, fatigue, and irritability. Fortunately, magnesium-rich foods like nuts, seeds, whole grains, and leafy greens can help keep you feeling balanced!

A diet that neglects balance not only hampers your immediate well-being but can also pave the way for long-term health issues like obesity and metabolic syndrome. Relying too heavily on processed, high-calorie foods while ignoring nutrient-dense options can lead to weight gain, insulin resistance, and a host of other complications. By embracing the idea of a balanced diet, you're not just improving your diet, you're enhancing your life!

Always Consult a Doctor

When it comes to your health and well-being, consulting a doctor about supplements can make all the difference. With dietary supplements gaining popularity, it's crucial to remember that not every supplement is right for everyone. Each of our bodies has unique needs, and a healthcare professional can help you navigate this complex landscape. They'll assess your individual requirements, pinpoint any deficiencies, and recommend safe, effective supplements tailored just for you. This personalised approach ensures you're maximising health benefits while avoiding the risks that come with unnecessary or inappropriate supplementation.

Why is this consultation so important? Because our nutritional needs are as unique as we are! Factors such as age, gender, medical history, and lifestyle all play a role in determining which vitamins and minerals your body craves. For example, postmenopausal women often need extra calcium and vitamin D to keep their bones strong, while vegetarians or vegans might require vitamin B12, as it's primarily found in animal products. By analysing your diet, health history, and, if needed, conducting lab tests, a healthcare provider can pinpoint exactly what you need.

Moreover, jumping into supplements without professional guidance can lead to overdoing it, which can be downright dangerous. Many people fall into the trap of thinking that "more is better" when it comes to vitamins and minerals, but this assumption can backfire. Too much of certain nutrients might cause toxicity or other health issues. For instance, excessive vitamin A can harm your liver, while too much iron can upset your stomach and may be risky for those with conditions like hemochromatosis. A doctor will ensure you're taking the right amounts, protecting you from the pitfalls of over-supplementation.

Interactions with medications are another crucial reason to consult a professional. Some supplements can interfere with prescribed drugs, diminishing their effectiveness or causing adverse effects. For example, vitamin K can clash with blood-thinning medications, and large doses of calcium might reduce how well certain antibiotics work. If you're on medication, a healthcare provider can help identify any potential interactions, adjusting your supplement plan to keep you safe especially vital if you already have chronic conditions that heighten your risk.

But here's another thought: do you even need supplements in the first place? Many nutrient deficiencies can often be tackled just by making dietary changes. If you're low on magnesium, for instance, simply adding more nuts, seeds, and leafy greens could do the trick. Similarly, increasing your intake of fatty fish or soaking up some sunlight could boost your vitamin D levels without the need for pills. A doctor or registered dietitian can guide you in making these adjustments, suggesting supplements only when absolutely necessary.

When you meet with your doctor, come prepared to share your complete health story. Talk about your diet, any medications or supplements you're currently taking, and any health concerns you may have. For instance, if you often feel fatigued, they might investigate whether a vitamin B12 or iron deficiency is at play. This information allows them to create a tailored plan that addresses your specific needs, ensuring you're on the right track.

It's also vital to acknowledge that not all supplements are created equal. Unlike prescription medications, dietary supplements often lack rigorous testing and regulation. This means some products could contain unwanted contaminants or boast dosages that don't match what's on the label. A knowledgeable doctor can recommend trustworthy brands that meet high safety and quality standards. They can also help you decode supplement labels, ensuring you choose products aligned with your health goals.

For those facing specific health challenges such as pregnancy, chronic illnesses, or recovery from surgery, consulting a doctor about supplements is especially crucial. Pregnancy heightens the need for certain nutrients, and taking the wrong supplements or incorrect doses can jeopardise both the mother and baby. Likewise, individuals with conditions like diabetes, kidney disease, or autoimmune disorders may have specific nutritional requirements that necessitate careful management under medical supervision.

Ultimately, talking to a doctor about supplements promotes a holistic view of health. Remember, supplements should never replace a balanced diet, exercise, and other healthy lifestyle habits. A healthcare provider can help you see the bigger picture, empowering you to cultivate a truly healthy lifestyle. So, when in doubt, reach out to a professional!

Chapter 12: Staying Consistent

Embarking on a journey towards better health is much like setting sail on an exciting adventure. At the core of this voyage are commitment and focus, two vital qualities that can steer you towards a healthier and more fulfilling life. While the allure of quick fixes and rapid results can be tempting, true transformation requires consistency, patience, and a deep-seated dedication. By reinforcing these principles, you're not just working towards your goals; you're also laying the groundwork for sustainable habits that will enrich your life for years to come.

The first step to maintaining that commitment? Understanding the "why" behind your health goals. When your motivation is rooted solely in superficial outcomes like achieving a specific weight or fitting into a particular outfit, it's easy to lose sight of your purpose. Instead, connect your aspirations to deeper values. Maybe it's about having the energy to run around with your children, reducing the risk of chronic illnesses, or simply feeling more confident in your own skin. Take a moment to write down these compelling reasons and revisit them regularly. They will serve as a powerful reminder that your health journey is truly worth the effort.

Next up, let's talk about setting realistic expectations. It's all too common to overestimate how quickly we want to see results, which can lead to frustration when progress feels slow. Embrace the notion that small, steady steps accumulate into significant changes over time. Losing just one or two pounds a week, gradually increasing your endurance, or incorporating one healthy meal choice each day may not sound groundbreaking, but they create momentum that leads to remarkable results. Remember, it's not about being perfect; it's about making progress.

Creating a structured plan is another key ingredient to your success. Long-term goals like shedding 30 pounds or training for a marathon can feel daunting without a clear path forward. Break these larger ambitions into smaller, actionable steps to make them feel more achievable. If your aim is to lose weight, start with simple changes: drink more water, reduce portion sizes, or add a few extra minutes of movement to your day. And don't forget to celebrate every milestone! Those small victories will reinforce your progress and keep your motivation soaring.

Discipline is your ally on this journey, particularly when the going gets tough. While motivation might spark enthusiasm at the beginning of your health journey, it can fade when life becomes hectic or results don't arrive quickly. That's where discipline comes into play, it's the commitment to keep showing up for yourself, even on those tough days. Build discipline by establishing habits and routines that make healthy choices feel automatic. Set aside dedicated time for exercise, plan your meals ahead of time, or stock up on nutritious snacks to make staying on track easier.

Remember, setbacks are simply part of the journey. Whether you indulge in one too many treats, miss a workout, or face a period of low motivation, these moments don't define your success. What matters most is how you respond. Instead of viewing setbacks as failures, embrace them as opportunities for growth and learning. Take time to reflect on what triggered the setback and how you can approach similar situations differently in the future. Cultivating a mindset of self-compassion and resilience means those temporary bumps in the road won't derail your long-term progress.

Creating a supportive environment can significantly bolster your commitment to your health goals. Surround yourself with encouraging friends, family, or a community of like-minded individuals. Share your aspirations and celebrate one another's victories, this collective cheer can make your journey feel less daunting and much more joyful. Additionally, remove potential obstacles from your environment: keep unhealthy snacks out of sight and set up a dedicated workout space to help you stay focused.

Tracking your progress is a fantastic way to stay motivated and committed. Whether you log your meals, track workouts, or take regular measurements, documenting your journey allows you to see just how far you've come. This practice reveals what's working and what might need tweaking, enabling you to fine-tune your approach as needed. Reflect on your achievements, no matter how small, as they serve as a reminder that your hard work is paying off and will encourage you to press on.

Lastly, it's important to remain flexible and adaptable as you navigate life's changes. Your health goals should evolve alongside you, shifting as your circumstances do. If a busy schedule disrupts your usual workout routine, seek out shorter, more convenient exercises that fit into your day. Should your dietary preferences change, explore new ingredients and recipes that excite your palate. Think of your health journey as a dynamic process, an ever-evolving adventure rather than a set of rigid rules.

So, prepare yourself for the journey ahead! With commitment, focus, and the right mindset, you can harness the power to transform your life and achieve lasting health. Remember, it's all about progress, not perfection! Embarking on a journey towards better health is much like setting sail on an exciting adventure. At the core of this voyage are commitment and focus, two vital qualities that can steer you towards a healthier and more fulfilling life. While the allure of quick fixes and rapid results can be tempting, true transformation requires consistency, patience, and a deep-seated dedication. By reinforcing these principles, you're not just working towards your goals; you're also laying the groundwork for sustainable habits that will enrich your life for years to come.

Chapter 13: Having a Balanced Lifestyle Without Feeling Deprived

Finding a balanced lifestyle that doesn't leave you feeling deprived is all about harmonising health and enjoyment. It's not about cutting out everything you love; instead, it's about discovering ways to weave healthy habits into your daily life while still relishing the pleasures that make life enjoyable. A balanced approach empowers you to achieve your goals without feeling restricted, making your journey more sustainable and fulfilling. Here's how to create that balance in a fun and engaging way.

Shift Your Mindset

Begin by transforming your perspective! Instead of treating healthy living like a set of rigid rules, view it as an opportunity to nurture and care for your body. This positive outlook can turn healthy choices into empowering decisions rather than burdens. For example, instead of saying, "I can't have dessert," reframe it to, "I'm choosing to savour a smaller portion of dessert that satisfies my craving." Suddenly, you're not missing out, you're making conscious, enjoyable decisions!

Embrace Moderation

Next up is the art of moderation. You don't have to banish your favourite foods to live healthily. Focus on portion control and discover ways to indulge without going overboard. Love pizza? Go ahead and savour one or two slices paired with a fresh salad instead of devouring the whole pie. This way, you can enjoy the foods you adore while still making progress towards your goals.

Incorporate Variety

Keep things fresh by incorporating variety into your diet and lifestyle. Eating the same meals and doing the same workouts day after day can feel monotonous and lead to burnout. Spice it up by experimenting with different healthy foods, trying out new recipes, or joining a dance class. Get outdoors for activities like hiking or cycling, exploring new cuisines and workouts keeps you engaged and ensures you're nourishing your body with a wide range of nutrients.

Plan Ahead

Life can get busy, but that doesn't mean you need to compromise your health! Planning ahead is your best friend. Prepare meals in advance, keep healthy snacks at the ready, and schedule your workouts, and you'll be set to navigate those hectic days without succumbing to unhealthy convenience options. Remember, planning gives you a flexible framework that supports your goals while allowing room for spontaneity.

Add, Don't Subtract

Shift your focus from what you can't have to the wonderful, nutritious foods you can add to your meals. Picture vibrant vegetables, lean proteins, and healthy fats that make your plate not only satisfying but also nourishing. Instead of cutting out all snacks, reach for smart choices like fruit with nut butter or yoghurt with granola. When you focus on abundance, healthy living becomes a delightful experience rather than a restriction.

Listen to Your Body

Tune in to what your body is telling you! Pay attention to hunger and fullness cues and feed your body based on its needs, not external triggers like stress or boredom. This intuitive eating approach helps you build a healthier relationship with food and prevents overeating. The same goes for exercise, listen to your body's signals! If you need a break, take one, and choose activities that feel good instead of forcing yourself into a dull routine.

Build Flexibility

Flexibility is key in maintaining balance. Life is unpredictable, and sometimes things don't go as planned. Instead of feeling guilty about missing a workout or indulging in a rich meal, remind yourself that one moment doesn't define your entire journey. Embrace flexibility so you can adapt and move forward without feeling discouraged. For instance, if you miss your morning gym session, go for a brisk walk during your lunch break instead.

Prioritise Self-Care

Don't underestimate the power of self-care in your journey! Stress and burnout can hinder your healthy habits, making it essential to carve out time to relax and recharge. Whether you're meditating, journaling, or enjoying a quiet cup of tea, these moments help you feel centred and ready to make mindful choices. Remember, self-care is not a luxury; it's a necessity for your long-term well-being.

Celebrate Your Journey

Finally, take time to celebrate your progress. Focusing solely on the end goal can make healthy living feel like a chore. Instead, relish every step of the journey. Whether you cooked a delicious healthy meal, completed a challenging workout, or simply drank more water, acknowledge those little victories and let them inspire you to keep moving forward.

In essence, maintaining a balanced lifestyle is all about discovering what resonates with you while approaching health with a sense of joy and flexibility. By practising moderation, planning ahead, embracing variety and focusing on abundance, you can enjoy the journey to a healthier you!

Chapter 14: Self-reflection and Setting Goals

Self-reflection, goal setting, and adaptability are not just buzzwords; they're essential keys to unlocking long-term health and well-being, especially as your needs shift and evolve over time. Life is a dynamic journey, and so are your health requirements, priorities, and circumstances. By regularly evaluating your progress, reassessing your goals, and making necessary adjustments, you ensure that you remain aligned with your aspirations and continue to flourish. These practices empower you to stay motivated and agile, even when life throws challenges your way.

Let's start with self-reflection, the cornerstone of personal growth and an absolute must for your health journey. Taking a moment to evaluate your habits, achievements, and overall well-being can provide profound insights. It doesn't have to be a complex process; often, simple questions such as, "How do I feel physically and mentally?" or "Am I satisfied with my current lifestyle?" can lead to powerful discoveries. For instance, if you're feeling drained lately, it might signal the need to tweak your diet, enhance your sleep routine, or integrate more physical activity into your life. Self-reflection sharpens your awareness of both body and mind, allowing you to make informed decisions that propel you toward better health.

Now, let's dive into goal setting, an exciting opportunity to turn that self-reflection into actionable plans. Setting goals gives you a roadmap and ignites your focus for positive change. Remember, though, that not all goals are created equal. Effective goals should be SMART: Specific, Measurable, Achievable, Relevant, and Time-bound. Instead of the vague aspiration of "eating healthier," you could set a clear target like, "Include at least one serving of vegetables with every meal for the next two weeks."

This clarity not only helps you track your progress but also allows you to celebrate your successes along the way.

It's also essential to strike a balance between short-term and long-term goals. Short-term goals offer quick wins that keep your spirits high, while long-term goals give you something bigger to strive for. Consider a short-term target of drinking an extra glass of water each day versus a long-term ambition of lowering your cholesterol or preparing for a marathon. This balance keeps you engaged in the moment while paving the way for a healthier future.

As time passes, your health needs and circumstances will naturally change, making it crucial to adjust your goals. What works today might not be effective a year from now, and that's completely okay. For example, a young adult focusing on building strength may later prioritise flexibility and bone health. Major life events like starting a new job, having a baby, or recovering from an illness can also necessitate a revaluation of your goals. Embracing change and being willing to adapt ensures that your health plan remains relevant and effective.

When it comes to adjustment, think of it as fine-tuning rather than starting over. If a goal feels daunting or unrealistic, break it down into smaller, achievable steps. So, if committing to five workout sessions a week seems overwhelming, start with three and gradually build up as you gain confidence. And if a particular diet plan isn't suiting you, don't hesitate to explore different foods or approaches until you discover what truly works for you. The key is to see adjustments as part of the journey, not a setback.

Regularly revisiting your goals and progress is another vital piece of maintaining alignment with your evolving health needs.

Carving out time each month to reflect on your achievements and identify areas for improvement can keep you accountable and motivated. Celebrate every success, no matter how small, it all counts! And if obstacles arise, view them as opportunities for learning and growth. For instance, if you're struggling to stay consistent with exercise, consider trying new activities or teaming up with a friend for extra support.

Journaling can also be a powerful tool for ongoing self-reflection and goal setting. Writing down your thoughts, feelings, and experiences allows you to spot patterns and uncover areas for improvement. You might realise that your energy levels soar on days you enjoy a nutritious breakfast or that stress impacts your sleep quality. Journaling documents your journey, helping you appreciate how far you've come and where you want to go next.

Remember that self-reflection, goal setting, and adjustment are lifelong practices that enrich your health journey. Health isn't just a one-time achievement; it's an evolving adventure. By staying curious, flexible, and dedicated to personal growth, you can navigate life's twists and turns while prioritising your well-being. This approach not only helps you achieve your health goals but also deepens your connection with yourself and enhances your appreciation for the effort you invest in living a balanced, fulfilling life.

Chapter 15: Creating a Roadmap

Embarking on the journey to a healthier, more balanced life can feel daunting at first, but with the right mindset, tools, and strategies at your disposal, it transforms from a challenge into a deeply rewarding adventure. This book has provided you with a vibrant roadmap designed to guide you from where you are today to where you dream of being, empowering you to seize control of your health one step at a time. As we reflect on everything we've explored together, keep in mind that your journey is uniquely yours, let this roadmap inspire you to adapt it to fit your individual needs, circumstances, and goals.

Let's begin with the cornerstone of good health: nutrition. Understanding what you fuel your body with is essential. We've discussed how moving away from processed foods and embracing whole, nutrient-dense options can significantly impact your well-being. Processed foods are often packed with added sugars, unhealthy fats, and artificial ingredients that can disrupt your body and mind. In contrast, fresh fruits, vegetables, lean proteins, and wholesome grains provide the nourishment your body craves to truly thrive. Consider making small, manageable changes like switching to whole-grain bread or adding a rainbow of colourful veggies to your plate. With each swap, you're taking a step closer to a healthier diet.

Next, we delved into the power of habits and how they shape your daily life. Remember, change doesn't happen overnight; it's all about those small, consistent actions that lead to meaningful transformation. Identify one unhealthy habit you're ready to replace and approach it with gradual adjustments. For instance, if sugary drinks are your go-to, try replacing one serving a day with refreshing water or herbal tea. Over time, these little tweaks add up to significant progress. Keeping a journal to track your goals and milestones can enhance your accountability and allow you to celebrate every win, big or small.

Physical activity is another fundamental pillar of health, and we explored how to incorporate movement into your routine in ways that are enjoyable and sustainable. From cardio workouts to strength training and flexibility exercises, each form of activity offers unique benefits for both your body and mind. Start with something manageable like taking 20-minute walks three times a week and gradually increase your activity as you build confidence and strength. The best exercise is the one you enjoy, so find what makes you happy and stick with it!

Let's not forget about the vital roles of sleep and stress management in supporting your overall health. Prioritising quality sleep is crucial, and creating a soothing bedtime routine, limiting screen time, and establishing a regular sleep schedule can all lead to a remarkable boost in your energy, mood, and focus. Similarly, taking time to manage stress whether through mindfulness practices, deep breathing, or simply carving out some "me time" can effectively regulate cortisol levels, helping you fend off weight gain and mental fatigue. These habits will not only enhance your physical well-being but also bolster your emotional resilience and sense of happiness.

We also examined the importance of tuning into your body and being willing to adjust your health plan as your needs evolve. Self-reflection and goal setting are ongoing processes; regularly check in with yourself. Are your goals still aligned with your priorities? Is your current routine working for you? Flexibility is vital as life is ever-changing, and your health plan should reflect that. Don't hesitate to adapt your roadmap when needed, whether it's reshaping your exercise regimen, experimenting with new recipes, or reassessing your stress management strategies.

Finally, remember that supplements and professional guidance can enrich your journey when necessary. It's wise to consult with a doctor or dietitian to customise your supplementation, ensuring that you fill in any nutritional gaps without overdoing it. Keep in mind, supplements are not substitutes for a healthy diet; they're meant to complement your efforts as you strive to optimise your health.

As you reach the conclusion of this book, one vital message emerges: health is not merely a destination, it's a journey. It's about progress, not perfection. It's all about creating a lifestyle that resonates with you, one step at a time. Celebrate every victory, no matter how small, and don't let setbacks dishearten you. Every choice you make toward better health is an invaluable investment in your future happiness and well-being.

This roadmap is just your starting point, and the path ahead is yours to shape. Take the insights that resonate, adapt them to your life, and trust in your ability to implement positive changes. Patience, commitment, and the knowledge you've learned from this journey. Embrace the adventure ahead, and remember that every step forward, no matter how small, brings you closer to the healthiest, happiest version of yourself.